THE
DEARTH
OF
CONVERSIONS

Register This New Book

Benefits of Registering*

- ✓ FREE **replacements** of lost or damaged books
- ✓ FREE **audiobook** – *Pilgrim's Progress*, audiobook edition
- ✓ FREE information about new titles and other **freebies**

www.anekopress.com/new-book-registration

*See our website for requirements and limitations.

THE
DEARTH
OF
CONVERSIONS

AWAKENING THE CHURCH
TO A GREAT NEED

ANDREW MURRAY

We enjoy hearing from our readers. Please contact us at www.anekopress.com/questions-comments with any questions, comments, or suggestions.

The Dearth of Conversions
© 2022 by Aneko Press
All rights reserved. Published 2022.
All rights reserved. First edition 1897.
Revisions copyright 2022.

Please do not reproduce, store in a retrieval system, or transmit in any form or by any means – electronic, mechanical, photocopying, recording, or otherwise, without written permission from the publisher. Please contact us via www.AnekoPress.com for reprint and translation permissions.

Scripture quotations from The Authorized (King James) Version. Rights in the Authorized Version in the United Kingdom are vested in the Crown. Reproduced by permission of the Crown's patentee, Cambridge University Press.

Cover Designer: Jonathan Lewis
Editor: Paul Miller

Aneko Press
www.anekopress.com
Aneko Press, Life Sentence Publishing, and our logos are trademarks of
Life Sentence Publishing, Inc.
203 E. Birch Street
P.O. Box 652
Abbotsford, WI 54405

RELIGION / Christian Church / General
Paperback ISBN: 978-1-62245-729-8
eBook ISBN: 978-1-62245-730-4
10 9 8 7 6 5 4 3 2 1
Available where books are sold

CONTENTS

Ch. 1: The Evil 1

Ch. 2: What the Evil Means 11

Ch. 3: The Cause 21

Ch. 4: The Cure 35

Andrew Murray – A Brief Biography 47

Other Similar Titles 53

Chapter 1

THE EVIL

The *British Weekly* of December 10 had a leading article with the title, "Mark Rutherford on the Dearth of Modern Conversions." After quoting from the novelist, the writer endorses his opinion that conversions of the old-fashioned type are becoming rarer: "In churches that are both prosperous and enterprising, and whose praise is in all the land, conversions, of the old order at least, are unknown."

In answer to the question, "Can any explanation be given for this fact?" he reminds us of the influence of the Christian home and men who are led into the Christian life without any sudden conversion or turning point. He speaks of the shadow of Darwin resting upon the messenger of peace that leads people to expect more from slow evolution than from a sudden change.

"The spiritual expectations of the Christian church are restrained by the accepted idea, or at least the expectations, of those who give the keynote to the spirit and religious enterprise of our times." Materialistic views of sin have a part in hindering both effort and expectation.

Above all, the questions of the hour, along with the desire to be perfectly fair in his statement of the old doctrines, paralyze many preachers. The writer of the article continues: "The result is that he is often found carrying problems in biblical criticism and theology upon his aching heart rather than what his forefathers called the burden of souls. There is scarcely any place left in his thoughts for the growth of that faith that saw those frequent and remarkable conversions that were the glory of the last generation. The very soul of the present-day teacher seems to evaporate in the attempt to present impartial, painfully balanced, delicately conceived statements of the truth. Such statements, however necessary, never seem to profoundly stir the hearts of their hearers. The zeal, self-denial, and eager expectation that have been the human factors working together in that great evangelical movement seem to have exhausted themselves for the time. If the modern dearth (or lack) of conversions is to be stopped, the revival movements of the past will need a fresh replenishment from the divine spring that gave them birth."

A week later, in *The Christian*, a letter was published from Mr. Moody to *The New York Independent* on the same subject, though from a very different standpoint. It is a reference to a statement in a previous issue of that paper that "there were more than three thousand churches in the Congregational and Presbyterian bodies in the United States that did not report a single member added by profession of faith during the year." Mr. Moody writes, "Can this be true? The thought has taken such hold of me that I cannot get it out of my mind. It is almost enough to send a thrill of horror through the soul of every true Christian. Are we all going to sit still and let this thing continue? Should we not lift up our voice like a trumpet about this matter? What must the Son of God think of such a result of our labor as this?"

In an editorial on Mr. Moody's communication, the *Independent* explains that some allowance must be made for the new churches that were founded within the year from which no report could be expected, for small churches without a pastorate, and for those that failed to send up any report. It expresses disagreement with what Mr. Moody said in his letter about modern biblical criticism, the labor talks, and the politics that have found their way into the pulpit. It does not believe that these are the causes. Then it proceeds: "But with all this true, . . . Mr. Moody does well to be astonished and pained at the thousands of churches that reported not a single member added by profession of faith last year. It is enough to send a thrill of pain through the soul of every true Christian."

Then followed *A Call to Prayer and Work* by Mr. Moody about this. After referring to what has been stated above, he wrote, "During the remaining days of the year, let us all wait upon our Master for a special preparation for the coming winter. When the New Year comes, why should not every Christian church in America and England begin the season with a thirty-day series of gospel meetings? . . . If every church will simply answer this appeal with open doors and a warm response; if every pastor will apply himself to spend and be spent in the Master's service at this special season; if every church leader will give his sympathy and cooperation to the work, the church will have reason to remember January 1897, both in time and through eternity."

I have been surprised that these papers have not met with more response. In the *British Weekly* of December 24, two letters appeared, along with a short editorial on the subject. In the following edition of *The Christian*, there were four or five letters. I do not know what happened after that, but one would have thought that the terrible revelation would have influenced many to lift up their voices.

The matter appears to me to be one of such vital and tremendous interest that I feel urged to take up my pen and ask my fellow believers to join me in considering what these statements mean and how they are to be dealt with if any deliverance is to be expected.

Let me begin with a word of caution.

A Word of Caution

One great danger that I see is that we do not take time to realize the extent and the depth of the evil. Unless we wait upon God to show us its terrible meaning, and unless we are brought to the full conviction that nothing but a mighty intervention of God can restore to the church its main glory – the privilege, in the power of her Lord, of seeking and saving the lost – each of us will be ready with our different reasons for our lack of converting power and our solution for its recovery. The whole discussion may very possibly end in new controversy as to the best methods of healing the disease. It is only when we begin to see how deeply rooted and widespread the disease is that we will go in our helplessness to the

> It is only when we begin to see how deeply rooted the disease is that we will go in our helplessness to the Great Physician.

Great Physician – to Him who alone is able to restore to the church what it has lost.

Disagreement as to both cause and cure has already been seen. Mr. Moody, and with him the editor of *The Christian*, and one of its correspondents, thinks that higher criticism is one of the great causes of much of the evil. In substance, the editor of the *British Weekly* has said the same thing. The editor of the *Independent*, though, is sure that this is not the case. A correspondent in the *British Weekly* of December 24 goes further and says that the acceptance that higher criticism has met with in the church is just one of the major reasons why conversions should be looked for. He says, "The religious atmosphere is altered. There is less sulfur in it, and there is more light. The more extreme forms, at least, of extreme Calvinism are extinct, science is accepted, evolution is assimilated, and criticism has infused more oxygen; yet we are confronted with the fact of no conversions in our churches. The old gospel is preached with a clearness that has never been surpassed. Good and true men, penetrated with the love of Christ and full of fervor, spend their days in proclaiming eternal life by Jesus Christ: and yet, and yet – ."

There are evidently two current trends in the church. The first is the literary culture, or biblical or higher criticism. Some people regard it as the great cause of the evil, while others look to it with hope. The other danger is the thought that new efforts or new methods will help us.

Higher Criticism[1]

If the dearth (or scarcity) of conversions were only to be found in churches where higher criticism is accepted, we might be able to connect cause and effect. But what about the churches where higher criticism has never entered? What about the churches of thirty years ago before its name was heard?

The cause must be looked for deeper. It might be that the spirit of modern criticism is as much an effect as a cause – an indication of an evil that had entered, even where all was sound and orthodox, for it had its birth within the evangelical church. The root of the problem, of which the lack of conversions is a symptom, may be found among the most conservative as well as the more advanced schools of thought.

The other danger is the thought that new efforts or new methods will help us. Mr. Moody proposes in his letter that all the churches should be opened on Sunday

---

[1] Higher criticism, or biblical criticism, refers to looking at the Bible from what is basically a secular point of view (especially in the extreme)—to try to determine what the passage meant in the culture in which it was written, using outside sources to try to obtain the meaning of the text, often without consideration of the authority of Scripture and the supernatural. It is often considered a scholarly approach in which the Bible is not simply accepted for what is said in the Bible, but emphasis is given to human reasoning and explanation.

night for the preaching of the gospel. The editor of the *British Weekly* strongly supports the proposal, though not entirely for the same reason: "The time is past for two regular sermons on Sunday. Ministers cannot prepare such sermons as are demanded now to this extent."

Mr. Moody does well in summoning all churches to set to work and seek conversions at once, but the ministers, those who hold positions in the churches, and the congregations have in many cases become so accustomed to conversions being rare that in many cases they may be unwilling, afraid, or unfit to respond to the call. For evangelistic efforts to be successful, we need ministers and Christians who believe so much in conversion that they will sacrifice everything for it.

> For evangelistic efforts to be successful, we need Christians who believe so much in conversion that they will sacrifice everything for it.

It is not more work or different work that will bring the cure, but it is only a church converted from her present state of conformity to the world that will either seek or actually have true conversions – that will receive from God the power to turn people from the world to Christ.

Let all who pray for the awakening of God's church seriously pray that He would show us these three things regarding the evil we are speaking of: its real significance, its hidden causes, and its divine remedy. If we meditate and pray earnestly to look at this trouble in the light of God, then the sense of helplessness may indeed come upon us, but we will also realize that deliverance is possible and certain to those who will listen to God's voice.

Chapter 2

WHAT THE EVIL MEANS

When a physician takes charge of a patient, the first thing he seeks to know is the nature and extent of the evil he must deal with. That is why he spends so much time and thought on the careful observation of the symptoms. The success of the treatment depends entirely on the accuracy of the diagnosis.

Even so, in dealing with the great question of the lack of conversions in the church of Christ, it is not enough that we acknowledge the truth of what is said, or actively set out to specify what we think is the best way to bring about a change. If the church is to fully realize what is wrong with her condition, and if it is to find the path in which God alone can lead her out of it, then believers and ministers must be brought low before the Lord and seek Him, the Great Physician, to reveal and remove the sin and restore that conversion power that comes from Him alone.

Let us, then, in the spirit of humbling ourselves before God, and in dependence upon the Holy Spirit, ask God to show us what the allegation implies – that the church of Christ is losing the power of conversion, of bringing sinners to the Savior.

Just think what that must mean to the Son of God! He considers this work His main glory. He left the heavens to seek and save the lost. He died that He might have the power to bless us in turning away every one of us from our iniquities (Acts 3:26). He was exalted to God's throne to give *repentance and remission of sins* (Luke 24:47). The conversion of sinners is the one purpose of His death on Calvary and His life in glory. It is the purpose for which His church was incorporated as His body – that it might continue and carry out the work He had begun on earth, and now continues in heaven. It is the reason for which the Holy Spirit was given – that the disciples and the church might be *endued with power* (Luke 24:49) to accomplish the work. It is the one purpose for the church's existence and continuance here on earth.

See how in the account that the Holy Spirit gives us of the church at Pentecost that this is the outstanding feature, as it goes from strength to strength. *The same day there were added unto them about three thousand souls* (Acts 2:41). *The Lord added to the church daily such as should be saved* (Acts 2:47). *Many of them which heard the word believed; and the number of the men was about five thousand* (Acts 4:4). *And believers were the more added to the Lord, multitudes both of men and women* (Acts 5:14). *And the word of God increased; and the number of the disciples multiplied in Jerusalem greatly; and a great company of the priests were obedient to the faith* (Acts 6:7).

- **Samaria:** *And the people with one accord gave heed unto those things which Philip spake* (Acts 8:6).

- **Joppa:** *Many believed in the Lord* (Acts 9:42).

- **Caesarea:** *While Peter spake these words, the Holy Ghost fell on all them which heard the word* (Acts 10:44).

- **Antioch:** *And the hand of the Lord was with them: and a great number believed, and turned unto the Lord* (Acts 11:21).

And much people was added unto the Lord (Acts 11:24).

- **Iconium:** *[They] so spake, that a great multitude . . . believed* (Acts 14:1).

One cannot read these expressions without feeling that in a church born of the Holy Spirit, and when preaching in His power, conversion must be expected.

What a Terrible Contrast!

Three thousand churches in America without one convert during the year! And about Great Britain, the editor of the *British Weekly*, who would judge neither ignorantly nor harshly, testifies that "in churches that are both prosperous and enterprising, and whose praise is in all the land, conversions, of the old order at least, are unknown." And then, how many churches have only a rare conversion, if any are converted at all! How many churches are there in which, after a time of special effort, the complaint is heard that the converts do not remain!

The agent in conversions has been more the wisdom of man than the power of God. How many thousands of ministers, missionaries, and workers of many names there are who will all confess that the hopes with which they began their work have been bitterly disappointed!

There is not a question to which they would more desire to have a direct answer from heaven than this: What is needed that the power of the exalted Lord, in giving repentance, may be seen?

What can be the meaning of this? Is it some mysterious appointment of God under which we must be content to labor on without success? Is it that just as in the waves of the sea there is an ebb and a flow, and as in the changes of season and climate there are cycles of drought and rain and of storm and fair weather that we cannot prevent or escape – so if our lot falls upon a time of spiritual barrenness, we must quickly submit and endure?

Or is it really true that the Lord does indeed intend and expect us to have conversions all along, and that their scarcity is simply the indication of some terrible wrong that makes it impossible for Him to give them?

If the owner of a vineyard finds that his vines do not yield the quantity or quality of fruit he has a rightful reason to expect, even though he has carefully tended them, does he not at once regard it as the proof of some hidden evil? He knows that the vine listens unquestioningly to the law of nature and that there must be perfect correspondence between its inner state and the fruit it shows.

The measure of conversions God bestows upon His church is the exact index of His estimate of its spiritual health. If He were to bestow conversions out of proportion to its spiritual fitness, He would be confirming it in its self-contentment and making the discovery of its disease impossible. Just as pain in the body is a merciful provision to direct attention to some lurking danger in the system, so the scarcity of conversions is God's voice of warning.

God's Voice of Warning

The lack of conversions is God's voice of warning. It is an infallible witness to the church that its state is not pleasing to Him, that it is not answering its destiny, that it is on a downward path from which nothing can restore it except a full return to a life in His will.

The church consists of members. Its restoration must begin with that of individual members who take up and bear the burden of the whole. Let all who are willing to bear the burden take up the position that Joshua and the elders of Israel did when Israel was defeated before Ai: they fell upon their faces before the Lord (Joshua 7:6). Joshua cried with them: *O Lord, what shall I say, when Israel turneth their backs before their enemies? . . . And what wilt Thou do unto Thy great name?* (Joshua 7:8-9).

Israel had been brought into Canaan with God's assurance that it could conquer and cast out its enemies. It had entered the country solely on the faith of the promise and power of God. At Jericho it had received more than its brightest hopes could ever ask as a pledge of certain and universal victory. But what is this? A sudden and terrible defeat! What can it mean? It can mean nothing less than the destruction of Israel and the dishonor of God's holy name! No wonder they took refuge in the only thing they could do: they fell upon their faces before the Lord. Defeat must mean God's displeasure; it must mean some terrible hidden cause.

Today we hear from New York and London the terrible tidings of defeat – not in one place only, but confessedly throughout the ranks of the army of the living God. The church has lost its hold on the people. The church does not retain the young people who pass through its Sunday schools. The church has failed in meeting the increase of population. The church has large and flourishing congregations, but without new conversions. In its struggle with ungodliness, worldliness, and unbelief, the most earnest of the servants of Christ are the first everywhere to express their faith that they should expect mightier displays of Christ's power than they usually see.

Certainly there is reason for the whole church to fall on its face and cry as with one voice: *O Lord, what shall I say, when Israel turneth their backs before their enemies? . . . And what wilt Thou do unto Thy great name?* With its King exalted by God to give conversions, and with the Holy Spirit given as the power of God to ensure conversions, the church is with one consent confessing to the lack of conversions. It fails in the one object for which it exists. With all its learning, influence, and work, it broadly lacks the one thing that God asks, the one thing that can make it a real blessing to the world: there is a dearth of conversions.

> The church broadly lacks the one thing that God asks: there is a dearth of conversions.

When Israel was defeated, Joshua and the people knew it at once. There was no hiding it. Sadly, the church has so much to occupy it, so much to boast of, so many external signs of success and blessing, that its terrible defeats are hardly felt. If they were, everything would be cast aside and the people would cry out to God to show what it means and to ask how defeat may once again be changed into victory!

No wonder Mr. Moody cried out, "What must the Son of God think of such a result of our labor as this?" Let each one of us take that question and find time to meditate quietly upon it until we begin to feel how grieving and dishonoring to Him the condition of His church is. Let us think, pray, and wait until He shows us how we have, in this dearth of conversions, the infallible proof that there is something radically wrong – how nothing but a new reformation, given as former reformations from heaven, by Himself from heaven, in answer to the confession and the cry of His people, can restore the glory that has departed.

Chapter 3

THE CAUSE

Every effect must have a cause that is proportionate in extent and power to the result that has been produced. For this wrong – the church of Christ failing in the very thing for which it exists – there must be some cause found that is sufficient to account for its terrible and universal prevalence. If it is true that Christ is willing and longing to give conversions, and if it is true that the Holy Spirit is in the church with the very purpose of working conversions, then there must be something that grieves and dishonors Him that is the reason for the lack of conversions. Until the cause is found, confessed, and removed, it is vain to expect any change.

That the lack of conversions is accepted so easily, and that the wrong of this is so little mourned, is proof that there is a veil upon the heart (2 Corinthians 3:15). Some diseases render the patient unaware of his danger. Unless the church acknowledges that it has not realized what this lack of conversions means (and for that, an intervention of God is needed to identify its hidden cause) all our discussion will profit little.

Many answers may be given to the question of why there is such a lack of conversions, yet they may not reach to the root of the evil. We do not only need to have single branches removed, but the axe must be laid to the root of the tree (Matthew 3:10). The disease is long-standing and deep-seated. We need to learn of the hidden sin in the church that has robbed it of the power from on high with which it was endued.

The Hidden Sin of the Church

It is this that we need to know, and it is this that God can and will reveal as we wait on Him.

Even though very different answers may be given when we seek to search out that primary source of the wrong, God's Spirit can, through such variety of insight, lead us to find what, in His light, is the real truth that He wants us to know. In fact, there would be no more profitable exercise for every child of God who reads this than to think and to write down what he really considers to be the explanation of the lack of conversions, in every country and every church throughout the world, of this sign of true spiritual life and vigor. The effort would help us focus our attention on this matter, would help us realize the difficulty of the problem, and would lead us to a sense of ignorance – which would urge us to cry out to God for His teaching.

The simplest answer to which universal assent might be given by all evangelical Christians is this: the lack of conversions is due to nothing but the lack of the power of the Holy Spirit. The lack of fruit in the vine is due to the lack of a plentiful flow of healthy sap. The lack of fruit in the church can only be explained by the lack of a healthy spiritual life. The Spirit of God is not allowed to have the place and the power that belong to Him.

> The lack of fruit in the church can only be explained by the lack of a healthy spiritual life.

This answer, however, only leads to a new question: What is it that keeps the church from recognizing and accepting her high privilege of having the Spirit of God as her life and power?

The answer to this question is very simple too. There are only two powers or spirits by which people are ruled and by whose action everything on earth is run: the Spirit of God and the spirit of the world.

THE DEARTH OF CONVERSIONS

Whatsoever is not of the Spirit of God is of the spirit of the world. This rule has no exceptions. Wherever there is a lack of God's Spirit in the church, there the spirit of the world rules and acts. Wherever the acting of the Spirit of God is partial and faint, there can be no possible reason except that the spirit of the world, the spirit of our natural life, has usurped the place of the Spirit of God. This is true not only in the way of doing the things that are plainly sinful and ungodly, but much more in counterfeiting the work of the Spirit and in doing all that belongs to and looks like the worship and service of God, but in a manner that is of this world and not from above.

When the sons of Sceva sought to cast out an evil spirit in the name of Jesus, the possessed man prevailed against them (Acts 19:14–16). They had the form, but not the power. They called in the name of Jesus, but the spirit of this world was in them rather than the Spirit of God. The lack of power in the church in casting out evil spirits, in making men bow to Christ, and in securing conversions can be attributed to nothing but this: the church is working in the natural power of this world and its spirit rather than in the supernatural power of God's Spirit.

Evidence of the Presence of a Worldly Spirit

The external evidence of the presence of a worldly spirit can easily be named. Some people will quickly point to the methods resorted to for getting money for God's work. All the methods and devices adopted to secure contributions, to get help from fairs and entertainment, and to play upon the lower motives of pride or rivalry and of display or pleasure are simply manifestations of the spirit of the world. If people say they can see no harm in these things, they simply prove how little they expect the true motives of Christian liberality – love to Christ, faithful stewardship, and love to souls – to motivate the members of the church.

Others will speak of the way in which the pursuit of place or of pleasure and of riches and luxury prevails throughout the church, obliterating all distinction between those who profess to be living for eternity and those who admit that they seek their portion in this world.

Still others will point to the lack of holiness and love and the lack of humility and obedience as the sure indication of a life conformed to the world.

Yet there is one area in which the spirit of the world may be least expected or noticed, and yet its power is far more present and hurtful than in those areas already mentioned. It may indeed be that just because its presence is least suspected or feared, this may be the door through which it finds access, and what was meant by God to be the great power to fight to keep out or cast out of His church the spirit of the world can in reality become the enemy's strongest ally.

I am referring to the pulpit. It is impossible to speak too highly of the place of influence God meant it to have, and that it sometimes holds, as the channel for God's power in conversion and for drawing people out of the world. Divine light and guidance are needed to speak properly of the influence it actually does exert in multiplying or diminishing conversions and in advancing or conquering the spirit of the world. The pulpit is God's chosen channel for conversions. Any inquiry as to the lack of conversions must lead to it.

> The pulpit is God's chosen channel for conversions. Any inquiry as to the lack of conversions must lead to it.

God's Word has warned us very clearly against the danger of the spirit of the world in preaching. Paul writes to the Corinthians of two different styles of preaching and of the two styles of religion that they produce:

> *I, brethren, when I came to you, came not with excellency of speech or of wisdom; and my speech and my preaching was not with enticing words of man's wisdom, but in demonstration of the Spirit and of power, that your faith should not stand in the wisdom of men, but in the power of God. . . . Now we have received, not the spirit of this world, but the Spirit which is of God.*
> (1 Corinthians 2:1, 4–5, 12)

There is a type of preaching of the cross, of Bible truth, and of sound doctrine that uses enticing words of man's wisdom and so robs it of its power. Its effect is that the faith of the hearers stands only in the wisdom of men. The result is a faith and a religion that is feeble and short-lived.

There is another type of preaching that is not with excellency of speech or wisdom, but in the absence of what can attract and gratify the natural man, it is in demonstration of the Spirit and of power. Its fruit is a faith that stands in the power of God. The result is a religion that can stand and last because it has its root in the personal experience of the working of God Himself through the Holy Spirit. That which distinguishes the preacher – the demonstration of the Spirit and power in him – also becomes the distinguishing mark of his hearers, and it makes strong Christians.

Making Strong Christians

The demonstration of human wisdom will result, both in number and character, in lack of conversions. The spirit of the ministry reproduces itself in the church.

Let us pause and ask the question: Do we not have here the explanation of the lack of conversions? In our churches we boast of the wonderful combination of literary culture and evangelical fervor. Could it not be that the evangelical fervor is what we have inherited from our fathers, while the literary culture is what we primarily study, delight in, and offer to our hearers? No wonder that conversions are scarce!

It is not difficult to see why the danger of the spirit of the world entering here is especially great. There is no way for God to communicate the knowledge of Himself or His grace in thoughts and words except through the mind. God's Word comes to us with argument and appeal, but this argument and appeal appear as foolishness to the natural man, and they have no power except as they are inspired by the Holy Spirit. How near and how great is the temptation to trust the power of reasoning or the attraction of eloquence while the demonstration of the Spirit and His power is lacking!

Then, with the very source of the channel of converting grace weakened and poisoned in the pulpit, it is no wonder that it has no power to expose, condemn, and conquer the worldliness in the church! Conversions are the work of divine love wrestling with sinners through the means of its messengers, breathing its spirit and receiving its strength into them. The lack of conversions where the gospel is preached can mean nothing else than that the weapons of carnal and worldly wisdom have been substituted for those of the Spirit, which are mighty, through God, to the pulling down of strongholds (2 Corinthians 10:4).

The editor of the *British Weekly* writes: "The present writer has listened during the present year to perhaps twelve sermons by very young preachers, and in not one of them has he heard the faintest approximation to saving truth, the faintest indication of how a sinner might find the Savior."

A statement like this points us to one of the main reasons and causes of the existing evil. These young men were trained in the theological halls of our evangelical churches. Their literary taste was cultivated with zealous care. They were taught that men who are to be leaders of the people must be knowledgeable of all our modern thought. They were trained to study and think, and so they produce what would secure an intellectual audience.

The editor of the *British Weekly* strongly approves of the proposal to have only one intellectual sermon a Sunday, and he speaks of "an evangelistic service in the evening, with plenty of brightness and direct, fervent, gospel preaching, conducted in an informal way, with three or four to take part." He then adds, "Ministers cannot prepare two such sermons as are demanded now. . . . The great difficulty with many is that they have no real gospel to preach, and even among those who are truly evangelical ministers, the tendencies of the times have interfered so thoroughly that they continually address their congregations as if all of them were Christians!"

Is it not evident that ministers are not being trained to preach conversion sermons and that many are not ready or able to do so? They can preach a well-prepared morning sermon, but the direct gospel preaching must be relegated to the evening service and the three or four lay helpers who are to take part. It is certainly time for the evangelical church to awake to the awareness that it is not training men to preach the gospel.

Not Training Men for Direct Gospel Preaching

Our young men are not being trained to directly preach the gospel or to be the instruments of the Holy Spirit in conversion. *Excellency of speech* and *words of man's wisdom*, depth of thought, beauty of illustration, and the stirring of pleasing emotion are taking the place of the *demonstration of the Spirit and of power*. We certainly do not need to wonder at the scarcity of conversions when the church, in training young men for ministry, does not make their preparation for direct gospel preaching its primary goal!

Do we need to hesitate any longer in saying what the cause is of this terrible evil of a church that was established by God and provided with the necessary power to securing conversions failing of its purpose to such a large extent? There can be only one answer: something has taken the place that the Spirit of God was intended to have. That something can be nothing except the spirit of the world in some form or other.

> It is by the wisdom of words that the preaching of the cross is made of no effect.

The one form in which it has entered and obtained possession of the pulpit, which was intended to be the channel of the converting power, is the spirit of this world's wisdom. It is by the wisdom of words that the preaching of the cross is made of no effect (1 Corinthians 1:17).

This is not just an evil of yesterday's growth. Long before modern biblical criticism was heard of, when all was apparently sound and orthodox, even back to the time of the Reformation, its beginnings can be traced. Wherever God's truth is received into the mind, is studied, is expounded, or is held or contended for in any power except the power of God's Spirit, wherever our natural abilities are trusted to do the work of God's Spirit, there you have that very spirit of the world that rejected Christ. While affirming its faith in His truth most confidently, it refuses that absolute submission to His cross and dependence on His Spirit that He demands. The church of today is the child of the church of fifty years ago; its weakness today is only the manifestation of seeds of disease that were then present.

> The church of today is the child of the church of fifty years ago; its weakness today is the manifestation of seeds that were then present.

When Joshua cried to God in the agony of the defeat at Ai, God showed him its cause in something that he did not have the slightest idea of (Joshua 7). If the church is to find out what is really the origin of its failure, God may show to us what many of us never dreamed of. Let us beware of being too ready or too confident with our answers. I feel deeply how defective my own insight is into the disease of which we are discussing the symptoms. There are moments when, beyond what I have tried to express, there still seems to be a deeper answer.

We can ask the question, "But how did the spirit of the world get such an entrance into a church that was so wondrously born and led of the Spirit?" In finding the answer, I think we will be led to the cross of Christ. The cross, with its spirit and its fellowship, is too little known or accepted. The cross, as the crucifixion of self and the world, is not preached, practiced, or witnessed to in word and deed.

Let us plead for ourselves and others that God would show us whether, despite all its external prosperity, or perhaps on account of it, it is true that the lack of conversions is nothing but the simple, legitimate result of the spirit of the world taking the place of the Spirit of God.

Chapter 4

THE CURE

When a patient suffers from weakness due to some external cause, then sufficient fresh air, exercise, rest, or food is often all that is needed. But when there is disease, some specific change must be brought about before health and strength are restored. I think we must all agree that the dearth of conversions is not merely a sign of weakness that can be removed by turning to a new purpose or effort. There is disease in the system that nothing except a direct healing intervention of God can cast out.

Our question now is, "How can the cure be brought about, and what is the part each of us must take in seeking it?" May God the Holy Spirit give us the answer.

I think we must begin by realizing our unity with the whole body of Christ, taking up its need as our own, and bearing the burden of it before the Lord.

An intellectual acknowledgment of what is wrong is not enough; it must become to us a continual sorrow and heaviness of heart (Romans 9:2).

In many prayer meetings, conferences, and conventions, the lack of fruitfulness has been felt and mourned, and the cause of the evil has been sought out and confessed. In renewed consecration and faith, men have turned to God for the converting power – and have found it.

But in all this, as blessed as the results may have been, there was one thing still lacking. Confessing sin, laying hold of the promise, and experiencing the blessing was very much an individual thing, or was with reference to those who might be more directly influenced by the recipient of the new gift. Something more is needed. We must learn to realize the unity of the body.

> We must learn to be aware of the unity, of the body, and to confess the sin of the church as specifically as our own.

The Unity of the Body

We must learn to be aware of the unity, or solidarity, of the body, and to confess the sickness or sin of the church as a whole as specifically as our own. We must learn to wait, to pray, and to seek the faith to claim for the church we belong to, or for the church of Christ around us, the same blessing and power we have received or seek for ourselves.

As this is done, as the vicarious spirit of Christ's sacrifice lives in us, we will get free from ourselves, and the work for our prayer and faith to aim at will become larger and higher. I urge everyone who reads this to remember that just as every loyal person in this nation would feel dismayed at an unexpected national defeat in war, even though he might never go and fight, even so there should not be even one of us who thinks that the question of the lack of conversions is no special concern of our own. If we love Christ and His honor, if we love God's church and a perishing world, then let us take upon ourselves the burden of this unspeakable shame and sorrow of a church powerless to bless and led more by the spirit of the world than of Christ!

As the matter becomes the subject of thought and prayer, of preaching and discussion in ever-widening circles of sincere Christians, the first step toward a change will have been taken. When God sees His children jealous for His honor – not judging, but bearing the burden of the weak or erring – He will undoubtedly look down in compassion and listen to our cry.

After we realize our unity with the whole body of Christ, take up its need as our own, and bear the burden of it before the Lord, the conviction and confession of sin must follow.

In all our teaching on holiness, we continually insist on the truth that new and deeper conviction, with fuller confession, is the only way to larger blessing. What has been true of the individual is true of the body.

In the discussion on the dearth of conversions, there will be a danger that we will regard it as a strange, unaccountable lack of power caused by a slight deviation from the right path, or that we will attribute it to the errors of certain schools of thought. Instead, we need to see that it is simply and dreadfully true that He has forsaken us because we have forsaken Him. God says, *Hast thou not procured this unto thyself, in that thou hast forsaken the Lord thy God?* (Jeremiah 2:17). Nothing in earth or hell could hinder conversion in a church that is walking in God's will and is entirely given up to His Spirit.

I am afraid that when this matter of sin and guilt is discussed, not all will agree. There will be explanations and arguments to try to prove that the evil is not as bad as claimed. We will be reminded of how much good there is and how much cause we have for thanksgiving. True conviction of sin is not easy anytime, and it is only the work of God's Spirit. It is often hardest of all when God's church is strong in its outward religiousness and good works.

Let all who believe that sin is the cause of the lack of conversions hear God's voice to Joshua: *Neither will I be with you any more, except ye destroy the accursed from among you* (Joshua 7:12). Before God's presence in converting power can be restored, the accursed thing must be put away.

> Should not the scarcity of conversions in Christian churches become the one great sorrow of His people?

Let those who believe this give themselves to be consumed by it. Conversions are the one desire of the Son of God on earth. Should not the scarcity of conversions in Christian churches become the one great sorrow of His people?

The One Great Sorrow of His People

Those who are consumed by this passion to get rid of the accursed thing so that God's power in conversion will be displayed once again will find courage and will be strengthened to lift their voices and cry aloud until their voices are heard where now they have no access. Their testimony may be rejected by some, but it will awaken others.

It may prepare the way for some prophet whom God may send to awaken His sleeping church and to convince them to humble themselves and repent, or it may begin to burn like fire in some of the leaders of the churches, compelling them to gather their church in a solemn assembly (Joel 1:14) to ask the questions before God:

- Is it true that there is this dearth of conversions?
- And is it true that it is because the spirit of the world is more enthroned in our churches than the Spirit of God?

Come, and let us return unto the Lord our God (Hosea 6:1), and He will have mercy upon us.

After confession of sin has been made, then comes the solemn time when the decision has to be taken whether it will be put away in God's strength.

Many sins are confessed and mourned while the repentant person feels as if he is in chains. Questions will arise like these:

- Are we able to change our style of preaching and worship?
- Is there any hope of getting this terrible

power of the world cast out of pulpit and pew?

- Is a return possible to that Pentecostal stage when the preaching was not in enticing words of man's wisdom, but in demonstration of the Spirit and of power?

The more we think, the more impossible the change seems to be. Nothing less than a revolution is needed. Nothing less than an intervention of divine omnipotence will suffice. In bearing the burden of the sin of the church, believers will have to be brought to the same point as when they were personally led out of their lives of worldliness and impiety. They had to cast themselves on the power of their ascended Lord to find courage for a full consecration and for the assurance that it would be accepted by God and made true in their experience.

As we feel how impossible it is with men to convince the church of its danger or to bring about a change, we will be thrown upon God's power to find the grace and strength in Him for a testimony to what He has shown us and a hope that it will not be in vain.

All discussions on the lack of conversions will be profitless unless they lead to action. As we pray, we must offer ourselves to God to receive, bring about, and act out the answer. When we have confessed our sin and the sin of our people, we must rise up to destroy the Achan (Joshua 7). We must yield ourselves to be taught and stirred and used by God to awaken His church.

Our conscious feebleness and our limited influence do not need to be a hindrance. A little match or the smallest twigs may light the largest fire. God can use us to touch someone of wider influence. Let us simply and honestly give ourselves to bear the burden and sound the cry: "This cannot continue. A change must come. The dearth of conversions must cease. If we put away the evil, God will arise, and His enemies will be scattered" (Psalm 68:1).

If we are faithful as individuals and in our circle of work, and also take a part in bearing the need of the church and the world, God will, in His time, hear and help.

Above all, let us remember that there must be no compromise in this matter.

God will only be found when we seek Him with the whole heart (Jeremiah 29:13). If the converting Spirit is to return to the church in power, then the church will have to say about the work of conversion: *This one thing I do* (Philippians 3:13). If conversion is the one thing God seeks in His plan of redemption to bring people back to Himself; if it is the one thing the Son of God lived and died for – to draw all people out of this evil world to Himself; if it is the one thing the Holy Spirit seeks to work through the church – then certainly nothing less is needed than for the church to make this, in all its breadth of meaning, its one supreme aim: the conversion of sinners.

The church that puts this first, that in apostolic manner separates itself from the world and forsakes all trust in its own goodness or wisdom in order to wait on the power from heaven – that church will have conversions.

Conversions Again

We may be sure that there will be many attempts at compromise. People may turn to evangelistic agencies and special missions while the state of the church, as a whole, is left unchanged. In times past, God has given us evangelists to fill up what was lacking in the ministry. If He finds that the church and ministry benefit by it, in learning from them the secret of conversion preaching, He may continue and increase this much-needed gift.

However, if its effect is to strengthen the tendency for the ordinary ministry to devote itself to what is not direct conversion preaching, we dare not expect Him to give us what would become a curse to the church. Plans will be prepared and carried out for having the morning service with its literary culture to gratify the more intellectual, and giving the evening to gospel preaching. It cannot succeed permanently. Such a church will be as the woman before King Solomon who was willing to have the living child divided (1 Kings 3:26). She proved that she was not the mother. A church in which the children of the living God are not begotten is not the true mother, for there is no wholehearted devotion to the living child. It will only be the story over again of Isaac and Ishmael in Abraham's home. *What saith the scripture? Cast out the bondwoman and her son: for the son of the bondwoman shall not be heir with the son of the freewoman* (Galatians 4:30).

Each church must make conversions its one object so decidedly that even where the morning service is devoted to the building-up of believers, it must be felt that the converted ones are being guided to everything to which conversion gave the blessed entrance. When the preaching to God's people is a prophesying in the power of the Spirit, it will still be as of old: *If there come in one that believeth not, . . . the secrets of his heart* [will be] *made manifest; and so falling down on his face he will worship God, and report that God is in you of a truth* (1 Corinthians 14:24–25). A morning service for believers is, as a lasting measure, the only true preparation for an evening evangelistic service.

If ever the church, or one church, or any number of churches make conversions the one thing they desire of God, and if they surrender to Him to search out and remove every cause of defeat, He will undoubtedly give it to them.

The church in the mission field is dependent on the church at home. When the problem of the lack of conversions is solved in the mother churches, the effect will be immediately apparent there. It will not do to pray for Spirit-filled missionaries abroad while our trust is in a cultured ministry at home. We must learn that the ministry within the church needs the baptism of the Spirit as indispensably as the beloved brethren who go to fight the darkness of heathenism. The battle at home with unbelief, worldliness, and gospel-hardened formality is not one bit easier, and is possibly more difficult, than that with heathendom. Here, as there, nothing can help us except God's presence and power.

Beloved brethren, the evil is greater than any of us can imagine, and the work we must do in seeking and preparing the way for deliverance is more difficult than we can think. If we are to carry this burden as we should, and if we are to help to awaken the church to understanding, confession, repentance, and casting out what has made this dearth of conversions a divine necessity, we will need to wait much on God for His Spirit to teach and strengthen us.

I pray that even these feeble words may be used by Him to reach some hearts and increase the number who, with Joshua, fall on their faces and cry, *O Lord, what shall I say when Israel turneth their backs before their enemies!* (Joshua 7:8). May we be found there until He says to us, *Get thee up. . . . Israel hath sinned. . . . You cannot stand before your enemies until you take away the accursed thing from among you* (Joshua 7:10–11, 13).

ANDREW MURRAY – A BRIEF BIOGRAPHY

Andrew Murray had a rich religious ancestry. His grandfather (Andrew) left the occupation of being a shepherd in order to work in the flour mills of Scotland. He was a godly man, and his deathbed prayers influenced his son John to enter the work of the ministry. John became an ordained minister in Scotland. John's younger brother, Andrew, became licensed in the Church of Scotland and was ordained by the Presbytery of Aberdeen. He became a missionary with the Dutch Reformed Church in South Africa.

While in South Africa, Andrew met the woman who would be come his wife – Maria Susanna Stegmann. She was of German ancestry, and her great-grandfather was a Huguenot who had been driven out of France when the Edict of Nantes, which had granted the French Protestants some religious liberty, was revoked. Andrew and Susanna's first son was named John, and their second son, Andrew, is the subject of this brief biography and the author of this book.

Andrew Murray was born in South Africa on May 9, 1828. His father often read stories of revivals to his family. When Andrew was ten years old, he and his brother John were sent to Scotland to be educated. They stayed with their uncle John, the Scottish minister. In 1840, William Burns, the revivalist, spoke in Aberdeen, Scotland. He stayed with their uncle John while there, and Burns' preaching, along with his long, impassioned prayers for revival and the salvation of the lost greatly impacted young Andrew.

Andrew and John went on to attend Marischal College in Aberdeen when Andrew was almost seventeen years old, from which they graduated with the master of arts degree in 1845. From there they studied theology and refreshed themselves in the Dutch language at the University of Utrecht in Holland. Rationalism was popular then. Mr. Murray in South Africa had written to his sons in Holland to be careful of the teaching. In a letter to his sons, dated April 23, 1845, he wrote: "You may soon hear sentiments broached among the students, and even by professors, on theological subjects which may startle you, but be cautious in receiving them, by whatever names or number of names they may be supported. Try to act like the noble Bereans (Acts 17:11). By studying your Bibles and your own hearts I doubt not, under the guidance of the blessed Spirit, you will be led into all truth. . . . Whatever books may be recommended to you, be sure not to neglect the study of the Holy Scriptures. This must be a daily exercise, and must be attended to with humility and much prayer for the guidance of the Holy Spirit."

Reminiscent of George Whitefield and the Wesleys and their Holy Club at Oxford, the Murray brothers joined a similar group at the University of Utrecht. It was called *Sechor Dabar* (Remember the Word), and its purpose was "to promote the study of the subjects required for the ministerial calling in the spirit of the Revival." The members of this group were often mocked, but they desired to live fully for God. On May 9, 1848, John and Andrew Murray were ordained by the Hague Committee of the Dutch Reformed Church, and they returned to South Africa to begin their ministry work.

At the age of twenty-one, Andrew was given the responsibility of being the only minister in a 50,000 square-mile territory in remote South Africa. For weeks at a time, Andrew would ride on horseback to preach to the Dutch-speaking farmers. Andrew married

Emma Rutherford, the daughter of an English pastor, in 1856. They had eight children together – four boys and four girls.

In 1860, Andrew Murray accepted the pastorate of a church in Worcester, South Africa, where they heard some speakers tell stories of revivals in North American and Europe. Murray and others prayed earnestly for revival, and experienced somewhat of a revival, though not as Murray had expected. He became increasingly interested in sanctification and what is now commonly called "the holiness movement."

Andrew Murray became the pastor of a church in Cape Town in 1864, and then became a pastor in Wellington in 1877. Also in 1877, Murray traveled to the United States and spent five weeks learning about Sunday schools, Moody's revivals, and the Dutch Reformed Church in America. Murray also attended the Presbyterian Council in Scotland and spoke elsewhere throughout the land, including visits to Holland and Germany.

Murray returned to South Africa where he became increasingly involved in Christian education and in training people for ministry. Murray's speaking schedule over the past few years led to an interesting and influential time in his life. His voice toward the end of 1879 began to be strained, and this difficulty continued for about two years, where he was not often able to speak publicly. He would write out his message at times, and it would be read to the congregation by others. Andrew tried visiting various doctors, traveling to drier climates, and more, but his throat did not improve. He did spend more time studying and writing, though.

After finding only temporary and inadequate improvements, Andrew Murray began studying more about healing by faith. In 1881, Murray was in London. He had wanted to be able to go to Switzerland to visit with a man he had met earlier in life and who was now the head of an institute for faith healing. Murray learned that this man, Otto Stockmaier, was then in London. They met together and discussed biblical passages related to healing and faith. Stockmaier urged Murray to attend the meetings of an American, Dr. Boardman, who had written on the topic of healing by faith and who then had an institute in London. Murray visited the institute and remained there for three weeks. He was taught that healing by faith was not just to heal the body, but to help one on to holiness and a life of consecration to God.

Murray's voice improved, and he wrote and spoke much on healing by faith after that. He did occasionally have less serious voice trouble later in life at times, and seemed not to place such an emphasis on healing by faith for everyone, but his experience and study certainly caused him to believe in the power and possibility of healing by faith for the rest of his life.

Andrew Murray continued writing and speaking. He was a speaker at the famous annual holiness Keswick conference. He was chosen to be the moderator of his church synod six different times. He wrote over 200 books and pamphlets, many on holiness and the deeper life. His books include *Absolute Surrender*, *Humility*, *Abide in Christ*, *The Deeper Christian Life*, *The School of Obedience*, *Waiting on God*, *The Ministry of Intercession*, *The New Life*, *With Christ in the School of Prayer*, *The Two Covenants and the Second Blessing*, and more.

Andrew Murray spent his last moments on earth praying and rejoicing in the goodness of God. He passed from this life on January 18, 1917, at the age of eighty-eight.

OTHER SIMILAR TITLES

Lectures to My Students (Vol.1-3),
by Charles H. Spurgeon

"The solemn work of Christian ministry demands a man's all, and that all should be at its best. To engage in ministry halfheartedly is an insult to God and man. Sleep must leave our eyelids before men are allowed to perish. Yet we are all prone to sleep, and students, among the rest, are apt to act the part of the foolish virgins. Therefore, I have sought to speak out my whole soul in the hope that I might not create or foster any dullness in others, and to this end, my lectures are colloquial, familiar, full of anecdote, and often humorous. May He, in whose hand are the churches and their pastors, bless these words to younger brethren in the ministry, and if so, I will count it more than a full reward and will gratefully praise the Lord."

– Charles H. Spurgeon.

Available where books are sold.

The Greatest Fight,
by Charles H. Spurgeon

And my speech and my preaching was not with enticing words of human wisdom, but in demonstration of the Spirit and of power. – 1 Corinthians 2:4

This book examines three things that are of utmost importance in this fight of faith. The first is *our armory*, which is the inspired Word of God. The second is *our army*, the church of the living God, which we must lead under our Lord's command. The third is *our strength*, by which we wear the armor and use the sword.

Available where books are sold.

www.ingramcontent.com/pod-product-compliance
Lightning Source LLC
Chambersburg PA
CBHW052125070526
44586CB00016B/2089